The Wicklow Way

Jacquetta Megarry

with

Sandra Bardwell

Rucksack Readers

The Wicklow Way: a Rucksack Reader

Second and revised edition published in 2008 by Rucksack Readers, Landrick Lodge, Dunblane, FK15 0HY, UK

Telephone 01786 824 696 (+44 1786 824 696)
Fax 01786 825 090 (+44 1786 825 090)
Website **www.rucsacs.com**
Email **info@rucsacs.com**

Distributed in North America by Interlink Publishing, 46 Crosby Street, Northampton, Mass., 01060, USA (www.interlinkbooks.com)

© Text and photographs, Jacquetta Megarry and licensors, 2002-8: see page 63

The right of Jacquetta Megarry to be identified as the author of this work has been asserted by her in accordance with the Copyright, Designs and Patents Act 1988.

All rights reserved. No part of this publication may be reproduced, stored in a retrieval system, or transmitted in any form or by any means, electronic, mechanical, photocopying, recording or otherwise, without prior permission in writing from the publisher and copyright holders.

ISBN 978-1-898481-31-7

A CIP catalogue record for this book is available from the British Library.

Designed in Scotland by **WorkHorse** (www.workhorse.co.uk)

Printed in China by Hong Kong Graphics & Printing Ltd on waterproof, biodegradable paper

Maps in this book were created by WorkHorse from mapping in the first edition and original field research by the author (2002-8), and are based on data from Ordnance Survey Ireland under Permit No 8464
© Ordnance Survey Ireland and the Government of Ireland.

Publisher's note

You are responsible for your own safety and actions. The publisher cannot accept responsibility for ill-health or injury, however caused, nor for any damage (whether to property, livestock or persons) that might result from walkers' actions. Land in Ireland is privately owned. In no way does any mapping or text in this publication imply the existence of any Rights of Way.

All information was checked carefully prior to publication, but walkers are advised that routeing is liable to change. Follow local waymarking and seek reliable weather information before setting out: see page 62. Please also check the websites: **www.wicklowway.com** and **www.rucsacs.com/books/wlw/** and its forum page.

Feedback is welcome and will be rewarded.

We are grateful to readers for their comments and suggestions on the previous edition. All feedback will be followed up, and readers whose comments lead to changes will be entitled to claim a free copy of our next edition upon publication. Please send emails to **info@rucsacs.com**.

The Wicklow Way: contents

Introduction

The Wicklow Way is Ireland's longest established Waymarked Way. Its evolution continues under the influence of the Wicklow Uplands Council, and readers of this new edition will notice many improvements during the five years since our first.

Starting from Dublin, Ireland's capital and principal airport, it's a surprisingly accessible long-distance walk. With time to reflect on the varied scenery and a countryside steeped in history, you will start to see Ireland through different eyes.

The Way quickly leaves the city behind as it climbs into the granite mountains and sheltered glens of County Wicklow, the 'garden of Ireland'. The Dublin and Wicklow mountains are the island's largest upland area, with wild scenery that belies their modest altitude. The Way runs above Ireland's tallest waterfall, passing around the shoulder of Djouce to reach White Hill at 630 m (2100 ft), descending past a memorial to J B Malone, architect of the Way. Appropriately, this overlooks Lough Tay, which he regarded as 'the jewel of these hills'.

The Way then takes you to the superb Monastic City of Glendalough: see pages 20-25. After the waterfalls and oak woodlands of the Wicklow Mountains National Park, it then climbs the shoulder of Mullacor mountain and descends into the historic valley of Glenmalure, with its military road and derelict barracks. Beyond the Ow River it passes by the sonorous hills of Ballygobban, Sheilstown, Slieveroe, Ballycumber and Garryhoe.

From Tinahely, the Way meanders through lush farmlands before finishing at the tiny village of Clonegal, County Carlow. The southern section, with its narrow lanes and rolling hills, is in strong contrast with the grandeur of the Wicklow Mountains.

Lough Tay, seen from the Way

Part 1 Planning to walk the Way

If you are new to walking in Ireland, the Wicklow Way may surprise you. First, only four pubs actually lie on the Way: the Glendalough Hotel, Glenmalure Lodge (Drumgoff), the Dying Cow and Osborne's: see pages 57 and 60. This is a by-product of the Way's history: it was created as a walk through the Wicklow mountains, later extended southwards), rather than as a route that connects villages: see page 61. So at the end of most sections of the Way, you must walk to a village for accommodation, food and drink – unless you are camping and totally self-reliant. This increases the overall distance that you walk: see Tables 1 and 2 on pages 11 and 12.

Second, most of Ireland's Waymarked Ways involve a high proportion of road-walking, much higher than many visitors expect. Overall, about 28% of the Wicklow Way consists of road-walking, but in the southernmost section this rises to 63%. This partly reflects history: most Irish people used to live in dispersed small rural communities linked by tiny roads and tracks, moving about on foot or donkey. It also reflects the strength of private landowners and the difficulty of securing off-road access for walking.

Happily, some of the road-walking is along narrow winding country lanes with very little traffic. Nevertheless, be aware that a car may appear suddenly around a bend, it may be travelling too fast, and the driver may be oblivious to the possible presence of walkers. Ireland's record of road safety is poor. If there's a verge or path, use it: otherwise, always walk on the right so as to face oncoming traffic. If two vehicles need to pass each other, it may be prudent to wait in a wider section or climb up a verge. Remain alert. See and be seen.

Away from roads, the Way uses a number of historic footpaths, their very names evoking Irish history – boreens, green roads and mass paths: see page 62 for a glossary. Ireland's population fell drastically in the mid-19th century: see page 27. You'll see ruined buildings, abandoned schools and other signs of this depopulation.

Johnnie Fox's pub, Glencullen, dates from 1798

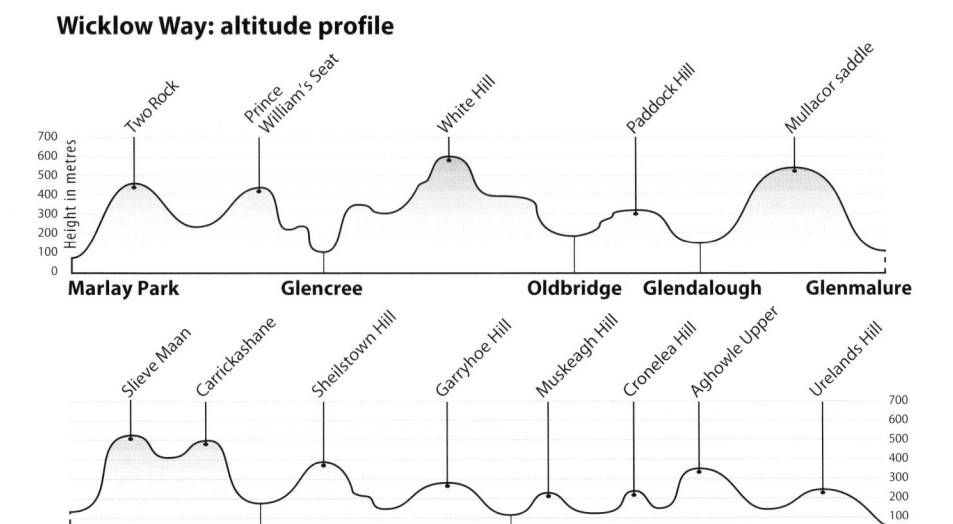

A typical boreen

Altitude, pace and waymarking

The Way goes no higher than 630 metres (2070 feet), so it's comparatively low-level. This makes it easy to underestimate. Unless you're a very fit walker, any expectation of rapid progress may prove unrealistic. In general, the Way crosses the lie of the land, so you often climb a ridge and descend to a valley only to climb another ridge immediately: see below for an altitude profile. Remember also that, especially in the wet, rough terrain reduces your average speed; and that a group travels at the speed of its slowest member. Overall, you are unlikely to average more than 3-4 km/hr unless you're seriously pushing yourself.

Wicklow Way: altitude profile

Height in metres

700
600
500
400
300
200
100
0

Two Rock · Prince William's Seat · White Hill · Paddock Hill · Mullacor saddle

Marlay Park   **Glencree**   **Oldbridge**   **Glendalough**   **Glenmalure**

Slieve Maan · Carrickashane · Sheilstown Hill · Garryhoe Hill · Muskeagh Hill · Cronelea Hill · Aghowle Upper · Urelands Hill

700
600
500
400
300
200
100
0

Glenmalure   **Iron Bridge**   **Tinahely**   **Clonegal**

The route is waymarked with a distinctive yellow icon and brown fingerposts. The quantity and quality of the waymarking has improved in recent years, with signs and information boards added for its 25-year jubilee in 2006. However, you still need to be vigilant over navigation. Waymarkers and signposts may be obscured by vegetation, used as rubbing-posts by animals, or taken away by souvenir-hunters. Sadly, marker posts may be removed or vandalised. Signposts arms are sometimes rotated, by the wind or by practical jokers: follow them only if they are consistent with your map-reading.

In places, it's easy to overshoot a turning. Should this happen, the key is to detect the error quickly. If you haven't seen a waymarker for 20-30 minutes, you are probably off the Way: backtrack and check your position from the map and printed directions. If you reach a completely unmarked junction, be very suspicious. Walkers who are over-confident or in a hurry are more likely to make mistakes than those who take time to check as they go.

Safety, weather and walking alone

No-one should undertake the Wicklow Way casually, because especially in the Wicklow mountains parts of the Way are very exposed, and run through largely uninhabited country. Even a minor accident can have major consequences if you can't get help. Walking in a group is considered safer, but if you decide to walk alone, think how you would handle an emergency, bearing in mind that mobile phone reception is patchy.

A major factor in planning is the Irish weather. Apart from a high probability of rain at any time, it is unpredictable year-round. On any given day, you may experience weather typical of any season, and perhaps of all four. This makes it especially important to have the right gear: without proper waterproofs, you are likely to become chilled or hypothermic, and with damp feet you may suffer serious blisters.

Well in advance of your first long walk, complete a few long day hikes, to test your footwear and fitness. If you haven't done much walking before, don't choose this as your first long walk unless you (or someone walking with you) can use a map and compass reliably. **Be aware that North is tilted by 15° on drop-down map panels 1 to 3, and by 35° on panels 4 and 5.**

Great Sugarloaf Mountain in winter

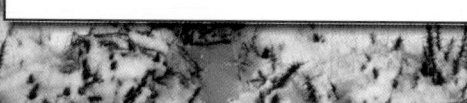

Mountain Code To report an accident, dial 999 or 112 and ask for Mountain Rescue.

Before you go

Learn the use of map and compass.

Know the weather signs and local forecast: see page 62.

Plan within your abilities.

Know simple first aid and the symptoms of exposure.

Know the mountain distress signals.

When you go

Never go alone.

Leave a note of your route, and report on your return.

Take windproofs, waterproofs and survival bag.

Take suitable map and compass, torch and food.

Wear suitable boots.

Take special care in winter

Dublin to Clonegal, or *vice versa*?

This book follows the traditional direction, from Marlay Park, Dublin, south-west to Clonegal. Existing sources nearly all describe it thus, mainly for historical reasons: see page 61. However, there are good reasons to consider walking it in the opposite direction:

• The more challenging terrain and wilder scenery are in the northern part of the Way, so it makes sense to tackle these later, when you are well into your stride.
• The prevailing wind is from the south-west, so you are (on average) more likely to have the wind at your back.

Most tour operators, and many experienced individuals, organise their walks northerly towards Dublin for exactly these reasons. There's a list of tour operators on page 62 and their websites can be helpful when considering itineraries. Bear in mind that the Wicklow Way's southernmost section is its least satisfactory: see pages 10-11.

Clonegal: the end or the beginning?

As an independent walker you'll need to decide:

• whether to begin your walk at Marlay Park and walk southward
• if walking northward, whether to begin at Clonegal or Tinahely: see below
• how to reach your starting-point from Dublin (where most people arrive by plane, ferry or train).

To reach Marlay Park, take Dublin Bus 16 from central Dublin to Grange Road, opposite Marlay Park north gate: it takes 50 minutes from O'Connell Street. An efficient Bus Éireann Expressway service can take you from Dublin Busarus (Store Street) to Kildavin or Bunclody (4 or 5.5 km from Clonegal), or direct to Tinahely: see Table 3 on page 14.

We describe the Way from Dublin to Clonegal southward (pages 34-60). We also point out where northbound walkers might need extra care with navigation. It's written not only for 'end-to-end' walkers, but also for those walking the Way in sections, for example over three weekends or as day walks. We give details of public transport on page 62, although support from a car and driver can certainly be very helpful. If using two cars, you could leave one at the end of a section, drive to the start and walk towards the other car, retrieving the first car later. Please park considerately: leaving cars in passing-places or obstructing gates annoys others and can be dangerous..

The southernmost section

Since the official terminus is Clonegal, it may seem subversive even to suggest that you aren't obliged either to start or finish there. However, many Wicklow Way tour operators and independent walkers instead begin or end their walk at Tinahely (and a few at Shillelagh). It's easy to see why:

• Tinahely-Clonegal is too far (31 km/20 miles) for most people to walk in a single day, but even less satisfactory when split into two: see below.

• This stretch has an excessive proportion of road-walking (63%, compared with 18% overall between Marlay Park and Tinahely). It's higher still if you add extra walking to overnight in Shillelagh. There is nowhere for walkers to stay in Clonegal, although there's a bunkhouse at Bunclody.

There are various options for tackling this section: please read pages 56-60 before deciding.

- Omit this section altogether, making Tinahely the terminus of your walk, which then comfortably fits inside six days.
- Start early, perhaps use our short-cut (see page 59) and/or accept a lift to bypass some road walking, completing the section in a single day.
- Spread it over two days, overnighting at Shillelagh (see page 58, third bullet), accepting the extra road walking (6 km) that this entails.
- Split your walk differently, avoiding an overnight at Tinahely, see Table 2.
- Book through a tour operator so as to cut out the road-walking and choose whichever itinerary fits the time you have available.

How long will it take?

Official sources give the Way's overall length as 132 km/82 miles, although the official halfway point is marked at only 63.5 km: see page 51. This sounds like a manageable week's walk, and most independent walkers tackle the Way over five to seven days, depending on the pace they find comfortable, whether they accept lifts with accommodation and whether they omit bits of road-walking or even the whole section south of Tinahely: see below. Tour operators offer packages lasting anywhere between five and ten days, a large range that reflects these issues.

Table 1
Sections, distances and villages

	Section	km	mi	nearest village	extra km	extra mi
Marlay Park						
	3·1	22	14	Enniskerry	5	3
Glencree River						
	3·2	18	11	Roundwood	3	2
Oldbridge						
	3·3	10	6	Laragh	2	1.2
Glendalough						
	3·4	16	10	Drumgoff	0	0
Glenmalure (Drumgoff)						
	3·5	14	8.5	Aughrim	9	5.5
Iron Bridge						
	3·6	21	13	Tinahely	2	1.2
Tinahely (Derry footbridge)						
	3·7	14	8.5	Shillelagh	2.5	1.5
Raheenakit (forest entrance)						
	3·7	17	11	Clonegal	0	0
Clonegal						
	Total	**132**	**82**		**23.5**	**14.8**

Purists may feel the need to walk every inch of the Way, whereas others may prefer to skip the boring bits. It's your holiday: set your own priorities. How long you need also depends on where you stay. Accommodation on and near the Way is scarce, whether bed & breakfast, hostels or campsites. Depending on where you overnight, there are sections where the nearest village with facilities may be up to 9 km away (5.5 miles). If you were to walk to and from each village shown in Table 1, your total distance could rise by 35% to 179 km/112 miles.

The extra walking is along a roadside, and oncoming traffic may make it unpleasant or dangerous. A tradition has grown up whereby many accommodation hosts provide lifts on request, perhaps making a small charge to cover fuel. (Such payments will be expected in cash: your host's car is unlikely to be insured for business use.) Whilst it is a great time-saver to be dropped on the Way to begin your day's walking, arranging for collection needs prior agreement about likely timing. You may also need to make a phone call as you approach the rendezvous, so you would either have to find a phone box or rely on a mobile phone.

The website **www.wicklowway.com** breaks the Way into seven sections of 12-22 km each (7.5-14 miles), similar to this book but overnighting at Moyne, rather than Tinahely. As of 2008 there were only two small B&Bs in or near Moyne, and although staying at either minimises the extra walking, this solution works only in season, and if you book far enough in advance.

Building on this approach, Table 2 shows a set of places where you could stay so as to minimise extra mileage. In practice, of course, you'd be very lucky to find space available with all of these hosts on the necessary dates, and there are many other fine B&Bs with excellent locations. Table 2 has been prepared solely to demonstrate that an independent walker can complete the Way without lifts, phone calls or excessive extra mileage. It underlines the advantages of booking ahead.

Table 2
Accommodation chosen to minimise extra distance

	Way (km)	Extra return distance (km)
Marlay Park		
	21	
Glencree Knockree Hostel		0.4
	21	
Oldbridge Wicklow Way Lodge		0
	9	
Glendalough Hostel		1
	18	
Drumgoff Glenmalure Lodge		0.2
	22	
Moyne Jigsaw Cottage		1
	19	
Stranakelly Lugnaquillia View		0
	22	
Clonegal		
Total distance walked 132 + 2.6		
135 km or 84 miles		

Whatever your approach, don't underestimate the time you need: if you are under pressure you will not have time to linger over wildlife or to enjoy the fine scenery. Consider allowing extra time for side-trips such as exploring around Glendalough (see pages 20-5), climbing some mountains, or even having a rest day.

Another factor, especially for keen gardeners, may be scheduling time to see Powerscourt House and Gardens: see the photograph below and the panel on page 38 for opening times. Although a couple of hours should be enough to visit the gardens, possibly the finest in Ireland, you also need time to get there from Enniskerry (or wherever you're staying).

Cathedral window, Glendalough

Triton Fountain, Powerscourt Gardens

Planning your travel

To plan your travel, consult the dropdown map together with Table 3. Relying on public transport makes it easier to return unassisted to your starting-point. If your group has a non-walking driver, he or she can arrange to rendezvous with hikers easily, because each day's walk has contact points with roads. Please be considerate about parking and use proper car parks wherever possible.

Table 3 shows scheduled times for bus and train (as of 2008); car journey times are the fastest likely within speed limits. Traffic in Dublin can be very slow at certain times of day, so these figures are only rough guidelines. Check schedules carefully in advance: not all services are daily, and winter timetables are often restricted: contact details are given on page 62.

Table 3
Transport options for reaching various parts of the Way from central Dublin

	km	mi	by bus	by car	by train
Marlay Park	10	6	50m Dublin Bus: 16 from O'Connell Street, Dublin	45m	
Enniskerry	20	12	1hr Dublin Bus: 44/C from Townsend Street, Dublin	45m	42m by frequent DART service to Bray, then bus 185 to Enniskerry (6 km)
Glendalough	45	28	1hr 30m St Kevins Bus: two buses daily, via Roundwood and Laragh	1hr	
Arklow (15 km from Aughrim)	65	40	1hr 30m Bus Éireann: frequent service daily	1hr	1hr 30m (about 3 trains daily)
Tinahely	80	50	1hr 50m Bus Éireann: only two direct buses per week	1hr 20m	
Kildavin (4 km from Clonegal) or **Bunclody** (5½ km from Clonegal)	90	56	about 2 hr Bus Éireann: two buses daily; Kildavin stop is on request	1hr 20m	

All times and frequencies are approximate, and liable to change. Check before making plans that depend on them; see contact details on page 62.

What is the best time of year?

Apart from winter, any time of year can be good. Always be prepared for cold, wet or windy weather and you may be pleasantly surprised. Consider the following:

- Mid-winter is unsuitable, because the days are so short: at this latitude, daylight lasts for only 7-9 hours in late December, leaving no margin for error.
- In winter, public transport is less frequent and you're less likely to see other hikers.
- In summer months, especially July/August, you may be troubled by biting pests such as midges and horse-flies.
- In summer, more tourists are seeking accommodation; however, in winter many B&Bs are closed for the season.

On balance, the ideal months are probably September/October and May/June. July and August are the busiest times for tourists.

Responsible walking

Common-sense and courtesy are a walker's best friends. You are a guest on somebody else's property, and should follow the Code: see panel below. The countryside provides a livelihood for its residents and is their workplace. You enter a farm at your own risk and are legally responsible for your own safety. You are responsible also for any damage to property, livestock or crops resulting from your actions.

Avoid approaching livestock. Your presence can cause stress to the animals. Never disturb pregnant ewes, nor approach young lambs, and give cattle a wide berth, especially if they are with young. In forests, be alert for local signage: Coillte (the forestry authority) sometimes has to post diversions for safety during felling operations.

Dogs

If you are walking the entire Way, we suggest you leave your dog behind. The Ways crosses fields grazed by cattle and sheep, and any dog seen chasing domestic animals is at risk of being shot. The access situation between walkers and landowners is delicate enough: you can help to avoid needless conflict. Taking a dog could also create difficulties over accommodation and meals.

> ### Code of conduct for walkers
> ✓ **Guard against all risk of fire.**
> ✓ **Leave all farm gates as you find them.**
> ✓ **Keep to the waymarked trail.**
> ✓ **Always use gates and stiles; avoid damage to fences, hedges and walls.**
> ✓ **Take all your litter home.**
> ✓ **Protect wildlife, plants and trees.**
> ✓ **Safeguard water supplies.**
> ✓ **Go carefully on country roads.**
> ✓ **Avoid making any unnecessary noise.**
> ✓ **Take heed of warning signs - they are there for your protection.**
> ✓ **Immediately report any damage caused by your actions to the farmer or landowner.**
> ✓ **Always keep children under close control and supervision.**
> ✓ **Please do not walk the Ways in large groups, which are seen as intrusive.**

Accommodation

There are various options for your overnight stays, depending on your budget, preferences and whether you prefer to walk all the way or to depend on lifts. Don't leave it too late, or you may end up walking much further than you intend. Booking is strongly advised.

Check **www.wicklowway.com** for accommodation, or use the services of a tour operator, or consider staying with a host who offers a Wicklow Way package, such as Lough Dan House: see pages 14 and 62.

Bed and breakfast or guest house accommodation is convenient for walkers who want a shower and a soft bed at the end of each day, and standards are generally high. Private bathroom facilities have almost become the norm, and breakfast can be a substantial meal. If a B&B displays the shamrock logo, it is registered with Fáilte Ireland (the Irish Tourist Board) and will be listed there: see page 61. However, there are many good B&Bs whose owners choose not to pay the affiliation fee. Unregistered establishments may vary more, but can be great value for money.

If your budget is tight, consider using hostels for at least some overnights. An Óige, the Irish Youth Hostel Association, runs three hostels on or near the Way: see page 62 for details. Hostels provide low-cost accommodation, often in small dormitories, with access to a communal kitchen and living room. Some have family rooms and en suite facilities. Hostels may not be staffed throughout the day, so check for any restrictions on your arrival time when booking.

Knockree Hostel is in a particularly fine location: see page 38. Due to re-open in 2008 as a 5-star hostel, it's much closer to the Way than any B&B, but you certainly need to book. Glendalough Hostel is also very near the Way, provides meals and is open all day. Sadly, there are no convenient hostels south of Glenmalure, so you either have to rely on B&Bs or camp.

Knockree Hostel, Glencree

The cheapest accommodation is, of course, that which you carry. If you are prepared to lug a tent, and cooking and sleeping equipment, you can be self-reliant. Camping is flexible, but remember that all Irish land is privately owned. Wild camping is not allowed in the Wicklow Mountains National Park, but may be permitted on open mountains or moorland. Sheep are wide-spread, so campers should purify their water. Be aware of the *Leave no Trace* campaign (**www.leavenotraceireland.org**). Follow the widely accepted *Camping Code*: see panel.

There is a commercial campsite with facilities near the Way at Roundwood: see page 62. Unless you are experienced in carrying heavy loads and pitching tents in uncertain weather conditions at the end of a hard day, you may find the Wicklow Way a tough proposition for a combined camping and walking holiday.

Camping Code

✓ **All Irish land is privately owned: ask permission before camping in an enclosed field.**

✓ **Camp out of sight of roads, houses and popular areas.**

✓ **Move on after one night.**

✓ **Keep groups small.**

✓ **Do not light open fires; handle stoves carefully.**

✓ **Avoid polluting water courses.**

✓ **Bury human waste thoroughly, at least 30 m from paths or water courses.**

✓ **Remove, do not bury, other litter.**

✓ **Leave the site as you found it, or better.**

Roundwood campsite
Adirondack shelter, Glenmalure: see page 49

What to bring

People vary widely in what they need for comfort. Before you set limits, be clear who is carrying your overnight stuff – you or a baggage handler – and the type of accommodation you use. This affects whether you need to pack items such as towels. If you are camping and are otherwise self-sufficient, consider using a baggage handler such as Wicklow Way Baggage to deal with your heavy items. To carry everything, you need to be strong, experienced and well-organised.

If you are booking through an operator, transferring your baggage between accommodations may be part of the package. If travelling independently, start by reviewing what you need for walking in comfort each day, bearing in mind the possibility of heavy rainfall. If the overnight extras are little more than a change of clothing and minimal toiletries, you may prefer to carry everything and remain self-sufficient.

Read over the checklist on pages 19-20 and think carefully about what to take. Do your shopping ahead of time. Once on the Way, opportunities to shop are very limited and supplies may be basic. Some accommodation hosts will provide packed lunches, which you should order in advance. Make sure you have enough to eat to last throughout each day's hiking. Tap water is generally safe to drink, but take water purifying drops or tablets if you will be camping or need to use water from streams. Take plenty of cash in euros.

If your arrangements rely on phone calls to your hosts, be aware that public telephones are scarce, and mobile phone reception is patchy. Whichever network you use, monitor the signal level whilst still on high ground: after descending to a valley, it's too late to discover that the signal has disappeared.

Notes for novices

If you have never tackled a long-distance walk before, welcome to a healthy and engrossing type of holiday. You don't need to spend a fortune on special gear, but suitable and well-tested walking boots are essential. If your footwear is inadequate, not only will you suffer needlessly, but you may also be unable to complete the Way at all. For advice on purchasing gear (including boots, rucksacks, gaiters, poles, a water carrier and blister treatment), please obtain our detailed *Notes for novices*: see page 62.

Ideally, try out a section of Wicklow Way as a day walk, if possible with somebody who is experienced. Other walkers are perhaps the best source of advice; if possible, join a walking club. Do several long walks before committing yourself to the Wicklow Way.

Packing checklist

The checklist below is divided into essential and desirable. Experienced walkers may disagree about what belongs to each category, but novices may appreciate a starting-point. Normally you will be wearing the first two or three items and carrying the rest in your rucksack.

Essential
* comfortable waterproof walking boots
* suitable clothing, including specialist walking socks
* gaiters to keep mud and water out of boots and off trouser legs
* hat (for warmth and/or sun protection), gloves and waterproofs
* water carrier and plenty of water (or purification tablets)
* food or snacks (depending on distance from next supply point)
* guidebook, map and compass
* blister treatment and first aid kit
* insect repellent: in summer months, expect midges (small biting insects) and/or horse-flies, notably in still weather
* toilet tissue (biodegradable)
* waterproof rucksack cover or liner, e.g. bin (garbage) bag
* enough cash in euros for the week.

Cash is suggested because credit cards are not always acceptable and cash points on the Way are scarce (in 2008, only Dublin, Roundwood and Tinahely). Bin bags have many uses, e.g. for storing wet clothing or preventing hypothermia: cut holes for your head and arms.

Desirable
* whistle and torch: essential if you are walking alone or hiking in winter
* pole(s)
* binoculars: useful for spotting wildlife
* camera: (lightweight and rugged); remember spare batteries and memory card(s)/film
* pouch or secure pockets: for keeping small items handy but safe
* sun and wind protection for eyes and skin
* water purification tablets or drops (essential if camping)
* spare socks: changing socks at lunchtime can relieve damp feet
* spare shoes (e.g. trainers), spare bootlaces
* notebook and pen.

If you are camping, you would need much more gear, including tent, sleeping gear, food, cooking stove and fuel.

2·1 Glendalough

Glendalough's Monastic City was founded in the seventh century in honour of St Kevin. It became a magnet for pilgrims for over a thousand years. The artist's impression below shows how it might have looked in its heyday, around 1150.

Glendalough means 'valley of two lakes'. From the Way, there's a superb view over this tranquil and sheltered glen: see the photograph on page 46. The confluence of the valleys of the Rivers Glendasan and Glenealo made this a natural site for settlement. Its dramatic scenery was formed in the Ice Age, and its steeply wooded slopes and valley floor provide a rich environment for flora and fauna.

The monastery was the centre of this settlement from the 7th century until the late 1530s, when the Irish monasteries were dissolved. For 900 years it provided a centre for learning, as well as for religion. Pilgrimages continued into the 19th century, notably on 3 June which is St Kevin's annual feast day. The site has been maintained by government agencies since 1869. Some of the buildings are superbly restored and maintained, others are ruins or barely discernible.

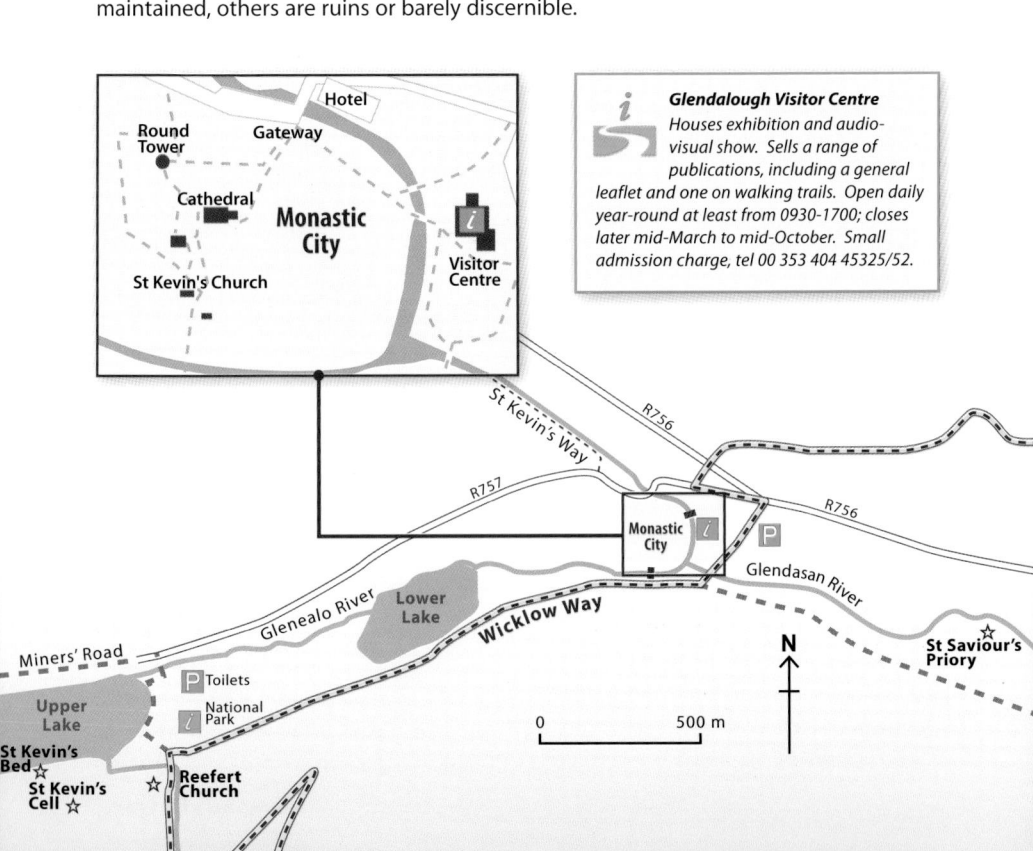

Glendalough Visitor Centre
Houses exhibition and audio-visual show. Sells a range of publications, including a general leaflet and one on walking trails. Open daily year-round at least from 0930-1700; closes later mid-March to mid-October. Small admission charge, tel 00 353 404 45325/52.

Artist's impression by Uto Hogerzeil: see page 63

Cathedral

Round Tower

St Kevin's Church

Gateway

21

St Kevin's Church (or 'Kitchen')

St Kevin was a descendant of the royal house of Leinster who turned his back on privilege. His solitary life as a hermit in a cave at Glendalough inspired many disciples, and the monastery was founded after his death in AD 618. It developed into a centre of learning, eventually housing up to 200 monks, who worked at copying and illuminating holy manuscripts, and caring for the sick. St Kevin allegedly lived from 498-618 AD, but in those days to have lived to an age of 120 years would certainly have required divine intervention!

Many other legends about his life survive: for example, when he was at prayer one day, a blackbird laid an egg in his hand. Such was his love of animals that he is supposed to have kept completely still until the egg had hatched.

Much later, in the mid-twelfth century, another saint, Laurence O'Toole, was Abbot of Glendalough. His buildings probably include St Saviour's Priory, with its romanesque windows and fine stone carvings of animals. Later, O'Toole became Archbishop of Dublin, and in 1226 he was canonised by the Pope.

Monolith cross, Glendalough

The Round Tower is surrounded by gravestones and dominates the scene. It stands some 30 metres high and is one of Ireland's finest. These tall tapering towers served both as a landmark for visitors and as a bell tower. Sometimes, especially when under attack from the Vikings, they also provided a secure place of refuge for people and valuables. Glendalough's round tower was divided internally into six storeys by timber floors. Once safely inside, the monks could pull up the access ladder. Its cap was rebuilt in 1876, using stones found inside.

Round Tower, with gravestones

Cathedral, seen from the east

Entrance gateway, with cross highlighted

The largest ruin is the roofless cathedral, which dominates the centre of the main graveyard. Built in phases, its nave is the oldest part, the chancel dating from the late 12th century, with beautiful stone carvings. Its walls are lined with grave slabs for people who died during a period of a thousand years.

The entrance gateway is imposing, and this is Ireland's only surviving example of a gateway into a monastic enclosure. Originally it was two-storeyed, with fine granite arches and a timber roof. Embedded in the stone wall is a stone tablet engraved with a large cross. This marked the boundary of the area of refuge.

The Wicklow Way enters the Monastic City across a footbridge from the south: see page 48. The first building you pass is St Kevin's Church, with twin steeply pitched roofs and a charming tower-like belfry. Its resemblance to a chimney gave it the nickname 'St Kevin's Kitchen'. Originally a two-storey building, its upper floor was probably used as living quarters, or to store manuscripts. Its date is uncertain, with sources claiming anything from 8th to 11th centuries. In the early 19th century, it was revived as a place of worship.

The reconstruction on page 21 shows only the Monastic City, which has the best-known buildings. There's a cluster of even earlier buildings about 1.5 km to the west, near the Upper Lake: see the sketch map on page 20. These include two churches, many crosses, and St Kevin's Cell and Bed, associated with the hermit stage of his life. The remains of two further churches lie to the east: Trinity Church stands on the roadside about 300 m east of the Visitor Centre, and St Saviour's Church, with its beautiful carvings, lies 1 km to the east, on the south bank of the Glendasan River.

The Miners' Road Walk and St Kevin's Way

For those with time to linger around Glendalough, there are several interesting walks: obtain the leaflet of colour-coded Walking Trails of Glendalough from the Visitor Centre: see page 20. The Miners' Road runs west for 4 km along the northern edge of the Upper Lake, to the miners' village at the end of the valley. Allow two hours from the Upper Lake car park for this round trip, which gives views of St Kevin's Bed and the ruined Teampall-na-Skellig (the Church of the Rock).

The junction of granite and schist in the rocks of Glendalough (see page 28) created rich veins of minerals, especially lead, but also copper, zinc and silver. During the 19th century up to 2000 people worked in these mines, with activity centred on the now-deserted miners' village. In 1856-7, the Mining Company of Ireland planted the fine stand of Scots pines that you walk past, intending them for pit props; but mining ended by about 1890, before the trees were ready to use. There was a revival in the 20th century, but the mines proved uneconomic and finally closed in 1950.

The waymarked St Kevin's Way links the village of Hollywood to the Monastic City Gateway, following St Kevin's likely route to Glendalough. It opened in 2001 and is 26 km long, following a mixture of forest tracks, riverside path and roadside walking.

2·2 History

In the early centuries AD, Ireland became the leading centre of Christian civilisation in western Europe, known as a land of saints and scholars. St Patrick arrived in the 5th century, later becoming Ireland's patron saint. Nowadays, parades still celebrate St Patrick's Day annually on 17 March.

Monastic cities flourished, and works of art such as the Book of Kells and Celtic high crosses were created. The Irish missionary St Colmcille (see page 54) spread Christianity to Scotland and elsewhere. From the late 8th century, this civilisation was threatened by Viking invaders, who were finally defeated at the Battle of Clontarf in 1014.

A longer-term threat emerged in the 12th century, when Anglo-Norman knights settled in Ireland. Led by Richard de Clare, they quickly took control, proclaiming Henry II of England as Overlord of Ireland. Their power slowly declined until, by the fifteenth century, the English crown ruled only Dublin and its surrounding area, known as the Pale. However, the Irish Parliament (dating from 1297) continued to meet until 1800.

The Protestant Reformation in England led to rebellion in Ireland, which remained Catholic. For over a century, English monarchs tried to control Ireland with a mixture of military force and Protestant settlement. This was pursued with particular violence by Oliver Cromwell during the period 1649-1652.

The 18th century brought prosperity to the Protestant landed gentry. Catholics, however, were denied basic rights in relation to property and voting, and were at an economic disadvantage. Demand for independence from the English crown began to build. In 1798 the United Irishmen rebelled, and Michael Dwyer (1772-1825) was one

View from Brusher Gate, one of Michael Dwyer's haunts

of their leaders. Active in many parts of County Wicklow, he defied capture for nearly three years while based in Glenmalure. Local people used to leave food for him at Brusher Gate: see page 44. Eventually, in 1804 he was sent to Botany Bay, Australia.

The 1798 rebellion was violently suppressed and 30,000 people were killed. The military road and Drumgoff Barracks date from this time. There's a good account of the Wicklow military road in a recent book (see page 61) and a photograph of the ruined barracks on page 51. In 1800 the Irish Parliament was dissolved and an Act of Parliament was passed making Ireland part of the United Kingdom.

In 1845 the Irish potato crop failed, and there were successive failures until 1851, leading to mass starvation. Over a million died and many more emigrated, mainly to the United States, some dying en route in the 'coffin ships'. The country's population, which had stood at over 8 million in 1841, had fallen to 4.5 million by 1901. Even today, although still increasing, it has not recovered to anywhere near its nineteenth century peak.

After the Famine, the nationalist movement became stronger. Charles Stuart Parnell's Home Rule Party achieved political dominance and Gladstone's Liberal Government tried to grant home rule to Ireland in the Bills of 1886 and 1893. This was so controversial that it split the Liberal Party and caused its defeat. By this time also, Protestant opinion in Northern Ireland was turning against independence, and the chance to create a united Ireland was lost.

In 1914, a third Home Rule bill was passed, but was suspended, a casualty of the First World War. Some Irish nationalists seized the chance of wartime to stage a rebellion. The Easter Rising of 1916 was put down swiftly and brutally. By executing its leaders, the British turned them into martyrs. After the War was over, reprisals by the Black-and-Tans (British para-militaries) increased the bitterness.

After the Anglo-Irish Treaty of 1921, the Irish Free State of 26 southern counties was established as separate from Northern Ireland. In the south, there followed Civil War between supporters of the Treaty and those, led by Eamonn de Valera, who wanted a united Ireland. The new 1937 constitution renamed the country Éire, but some links with Britain remained.

In 1948-9 Ireland severed these links and left the Commonwealth, changing its name to the Republic of Ireland. Independence did not bring prosperity at first, but the Republic escaped the sectarian troubles that have affected Northern Ireland. In 1973 it joined what is now the European Union. Economic development has since been rapid, and Ireland's standard of living is now in line with the best in western Europe.

2·3 Geology and scenery

Carrawaystick waterfall: schist and granite

The scenery you walk through on the Way is formed by very old rocks of four main types: granite, quartzite, schist and slate. Some valleys (especially Glendalough, Glenmalure and Glendasan) also have deposits of lead ore, or galena, which once supported mining. Samples of these five rocks are set into a display panel above Glendalough (see page 48).

Granite is formed when a rising intrusion of molten magma, deep under the earth's crust, cools slowly to form solid rock. After prolonged erosion removed the rocks above, eventually the granite was exposed. Crystals of quartz formed within it: the slower the cooling, the larger the crystals. The colour of granite varies in shades of grey, buff or light brown. Granite is a hard rock, and from the Way (especially its northern part) you will see many fine examples of granite outcrops and crags left prominent by erosion.

After a long period of weathering, granite breaks down to form various sands and clays. Quartzite is formed when the action of heat and pressure re-crystallises sand into rock. Great Sugarloaf mountain is a prominent quartzite landmark (see photograph on page 8), as is its smaller companion, Little Sugarloaf.

Some places on the Way show very obvious junctions between different rock types, often between granite and schist (the formation of which is explained on page 29). Compare, for example, the surfaces on either side of the waterfall in the photograph above: on the left is rough schist with loose scree, on the right is smoothly rounded granite.

Some 500 million years ago, the Wicklow area was at the bottom of a deep sea. Underneath it, accumulated layers of mud and sand were slowly compressed under enormous weight into layers of sedimentary rocks (mudstones and sandstones).

About 400 million years ago, the forerunner of what is now North America ploughed slowly into the continent now known as Europe. Colossal shock waves pushed molten magma up through the layers of sedimentary rocks, to form the Wicklow mountains, which are largely granite. All round the edges of this giant upthrust, immense heat and pressure-baked the sedimentary rocks, changing their state. This process created metamorphic ('changed') rocks such as schist and slate. Higher temperatures resulted in the formation of schist, whilst lower temperatures were linked with slate.

When schist and slate are enriched with shiny flecks of mica, they are called mica schist or mica slate. Powerscourt waterfall cascades down cliffs of mica schist (see page 40), and Knockree Hill is mica-rich schist with a band of quartzite. Mica in rocks tends to look shiny or silvery, but when suspended as tiny flakes in water, it creates the remarkable green colour seen in the photograph below.

Millions of years later, the land was thrust above the sea, and prolonged erosion stripped away schist, leaving the granite domes exposed. About 1.7 million years ago, the Ice Age began and glaciers up to 300 metres deep ground out the valleys, making them deeper and more rounded. The process continued throughout the Ice Ages, the last of which ended around 15,000 years ago.

In addition to re-shaping the valleys, the glaciers plucked masses of granite and schist from the valleys, and transported them over long distances, eventually depositing them as boulders and cobbles (known as erratics) wherever they melted. Erratics can mislead you about the underlying geology: Crone Woods has granite erratics deposited 15-20,000 years ago, but their bedrock is slate.

Mica-rich water in the plunge pool of Poulanass waterfall

Sometimes the moraine (mound of debris) deposited at the end of a glacier was large enough to act as a dam, forming a lake such as Lough Tay, created during the last Ice Age. As you walk down the Barr, overlooking Lough Tay, you may notice mica-rich schists boulders like the one below. There are also some extravagantly folded layers of quartzite.

Lough Tay, dammed by a glacier's moraine

Not all geological processes take so very long. When you stand between Glendalough's two lakes, it seems barely credible that only 9000 years ago the valley had only one lake. Over the centuries, Lugduff Brook brought down some 20 million tonnes of sand, mud and gravel, building up the plain (or *alluvial fan*) that now separates the two lakes. The Brook drops impressively from its hanging valley at Poulanass waterfall (see page 47), but it seems scarcely powerful enough to have created the huge land area between these lakes. Yet it did, and the process continues, gradually making the lakes shallower, until eventually they will be filled in.

Boulder of mica schist lying by the Way

2·4 Habitats and wildlife

Bell heather

The Wicklow Way runs
through three main types of
habitat, described below:
• upland
• woodland
• hedgerow.

To improve your chances of seeing wildlife, walk alone or with
others who share your interest, and are willing to move quietly. Try to
set off soon after sunrise, or go for a stroll in the evening, when animals
are more active. Since this applies to midges too, protect your skin thoroughly,
especially from May to September and in still weather. Carry binoculars if possible.

Famously, Ireland has no snakes. Allegedly they were driven out by St Patrick, but the
truth is more prosaic: there probably never were any on this island. However, it does
have its own sub-species, for example Irish jay and Irish hare, a relative of Arctic hare.

Upland

You may notice three kinds of heather: bell heather has deep purple flowers, ling
heather has pinker ones and cross-leaved heath has flowers in pale pink. Heather
flourishes on the soft upland schist, but not on hard granite: see page 28. Bilberry
associates with heather and belongs to the same family. Its purple berries are
attractive to many species, including humans. Known elsewhere as blueberry or
blaeberry, in Ireland the word is *fraughan*.

The Wicklow mountains are home to many birds: small upland birds include skylark
and meadow pipit. You may see glossy black raven and hear its harsh call 'pruk'.
Smaller birds of prey include merlin or peregrine falcon, recently recovering from the
threat of extinction posed by pesticides. Buzzard are larger birds of prey, easy to
recognise as they soar on air currents, wings held motionless in a shallow Vee. Red
kites had been extinct for 200 years until the Wicklow Red Kite Project successfully
introduced 30 birds from Wales in 2007.

Red grouse, a game bird that depends heavily on heather

Irish red grouse are distinct from the Scottish sub-species, and closer to the continental willow grouse. They breed in the heather-clad Wicklow mountains and depend heavily on a suitable age range in the heather, needing young shoots to feed on but taller plants for ground cover and nesting. If you disturb a red grouse, it may erupt with a whirring of wings, croaking its alarm call. Consider yourself lucky to see this threatened game bird, and back off to avoid any further disturbance.

Woodland

There is a delicate balance between the woodland habitat and the animals that depend on it for shelter, food and nesting sites. Since the extinction of the wolf, their major natural predator, deer population growth has been excessive, with over-grazing destroying habitat. Sadly, the native Irish red deer have interbred with sika deer imported to the Powerscourt estate in the 1860s, and the entire Wicklow population may now be hybrid. Around Glendalough, you will see high deer fences around exclosures – fenced-off areas that exclude deer and feral (wild) goats, so as to allow the vegetation to develop.

The Way goes through large areas of forest, nearly all comprising productive conifers such as sitka, lodgepole pine and European larch. Although not as rich in species as broadleaved woodland, these support some colourful birds such as crossbill, redpoll and siskin. Conifers are also home to the charming red squirrel: if you see chewed-up cones lying on the ground, look about for the red squirrels that may have been feeding on them recently.

There are small patches of semi-natural broadleaved woodland, especially around Glendalough. Look out for sessile oak, Ireland's national tree. To distinguish it from English oak, look at how the acorn is attached: if it sits directly on the branch, the oak is sessile, but if it hangs from a stalk (peduncle) it's English (pedunculate). Oak woodland is particularly rich in wildlife, supporting 200 different species of invertebrate.

Hedgerow

In spring or early summer, you will be struck by the rich variety in hedgerows and how much insect and bird life they support. Hedgerows form dense corridors of vegetation, based on a mixture of shrubs such as the white-flowering hawthorn (from May/June) and blackthorn (from March). They support climbers such as clematis and honeysuckle, interwoven with wild flowers such as dog rose, yellow primrose, purple foxglove and wild violet.

Sessile oak: young leaves at first blush

Most hedgerows are 150-200 years old, although some date back as far as the 16th century. They form borders to fields, green roads and boreens, and support a wide variety of insect life. Look out for bees, grasshoppers, flies, caterpillars and butterflies.

A wide range of birds feed on the insects and flowers. Look out for the tiny wren: you might glimpse its red-brown colour and rapid, darting flight. Song thrush, blackbird and robin are common. You will hear various warblers, and may see the colourful bullfinch or yellowhammer.

Insects flourish in hedgerows

3·1 Marlay Park to Glencree River

Map	**panel 1**
Distance	**22 kilometres (14 miles) to Glencree River**
Terrain	**mixture of road-walking (21%), forest tracks and hillside paths; parts can be wet underfoot**
Grade	**steady ascent to 490 metres, moderate descent into Glencullen, then further ascent to 470 metres, dropping steeply into Glencree**
Side-trips	**Powerscourt House and gardens**
Summary	**a varied day, ranging from pleasant wooded paths of Marlay Park to the young forests and open hillsides of the mountains and glens south of Dublin**

From Marlay Park's north entrance (Grange Road), cross the car park. Leaving Marlay House behind to your right, you'll face a Wicklow Way information board and stone wall marking its official starting-point. Pass over the low stone stile and follow the path across the lawns.

> **Marlay Park**
> *The park opens at 1000 all year, but closing time varies: 1700 November-January, 1800 February-March, 1900 in October, 2000 in April and September, and 2100 May to August. There are craft and coffee shops in the courtyard. Marlay House was built about 1794 by a Dublin banking family, the La Touches.*

THE WICKLOW WAY

- Follow the waymarkers generally southward through the park, which has fine mature trees, varied wildlife and attractive water features with formal bridges.

- Turn right to follow the perimeter path for about 700 m. Exit through the gates of the car park and turn right.

- Follow the concrete path between a high wall screening the golf course on your right and a lower wall screening the M50 motorway on your left.

- The path soon ends at a junction: cross the road to reach the pavement, turn left and walk through the underpass to a small roundabout with a waymarker.

- Bear left up the cul-de-sac (Kilmashogue Lane). You pass St Columba's College (founded in 1843) and the electric gates and security cameras of some opulent houses.

- About 1 km south of the roundabout, turn left along the waymarked lower of two roads and walk past the metal barrier into Kilmashogue Wood.

Marlay House, seen across the lawns

Marlay Park · 10 · 6 · R116 to Glencullen · 12 · 8 · Glencree River

- Follow the forest road, which twists and turns a bit, for about 3 km. In the open sections you will see wonderful views over Dublin and its harbour to the north-east. The cluster of masts to the east is on Three Rock mountain.

- Look out for the right turn up a narrow bouldery path, which climbs steeply for 250 m.

- Turn right as indicated, and shortly, at the T-junction where a wide view opens out, turn left to walk up the ridge of Two Rock mountain.

- After 750 m, the Way levels out and makes an obvious right turn downhill. Unless conditions are poor, instead divert left to reach the top of Two Rock (Fairy Castle on some maps). The payoff for this detour (500 m each way) is a panoramic view from the cairn, which covers a pre-historic grave.

The steep, bouldery path

You'll look down on the nearby masts of Three Rock, a spur of Two Rock. On a fine day, there's no better place for a picnic lunch.

- Follow the path down a spur to the edge of Tibradden Forest, with good views on both sides. To the south-west, a mast marks the summit of Kippure (757 m).

Kippure from the Way below Prince William's Seat

- After 1 km, turn left along the edge of some woods and go down the steep path that abruptly descends to the main road (R116): beware of fast-moving traffic.

- Turn left and walk gently downhill along the road for 1.6 km. Look out for the waymarker and signpost for Boranaraltry Lane, where you turn sharp right. (To visit Johnnie Fox's pub in Glencullen, instead keep straight on for 1.6 km. Its claim to be the highest pub in Ireland is spurious, but it serves great seafood and has antique charm: see its photograph, page 5.)

- Follow the lane downhill to the curved stone bridge and cross Glencullen River. Follow the road as it swings left and climbs out of the valley. The tarmac surface soon ends at a barrier.

- Pass through a gate into Glencullen Forest. Look out for the waymarker where the Way turns right uphill. Follow the waymarkers carefully, and after several uphill zigzags, you should be heading southerly, still climbing.

- From the edge of the forest, the Way crosses a stretch of heathery moorland on a constructed, well-drained path. Look out for a granite tor called Ravens Rock to the left and enjoy the distant views north-east to Dublin Bay and south-east to Great Sugarloaf mountain. The boundary between Dublin and Wicklow counties passes through Prince William's Seat (555 m), which is up on your right.

View from county boundary

- The Way descends into what remains of Curtlestown Wood. Look carefully for waymarkers in this section: in March 2008, recent clear felling had left little sign of a path except some splashes of pink and yellow paint on the rocks. These led clearly to a newly constructed path heading downhill through the felled area.

- After the path, keep straight ahead down a broad forest road that sweeps downhill in zigzags with open views, including Knockree Hill and Djouce to the south. Stay alert for waymarkers until you exit Curtlestown Wood at the public road.

- If staying in Enniskerry, follow this road for nearly 5 km to the left (east). From there, consider a visit to Powerscourt, south-west of the village, with a long walk up the drive: see panel, and the photograph on page 13. (You'll see its waterfall, 5 km further south-west, from the Way: see page 40.)

> ### Powerscourt gardens
> *Superb blend of formal gardens, ornamental lakes and romantic backdrop of Great Sugarloaf mountain, with some 200 varieties of trees and shrubs. The mansion's interior was burned out in 1974 and houses an exhibition. Open daily 0930-1730 in summer, admission charges; see www.powerscourt.ie*

- To continue the Way, instead turn right at the road. (For Coolakay House, keep going until you reach page 40, fourth bullet.)

- After 200 m, the main road swings right but the Way bears left up the minor road signposted for Knockree Hostel. Follow it for 800 m to the car park where you turn left.

- Enter the forest and follow the track as it climbs the shoulder of Knockree Hill (342 m). To your right across the glen you can see the hills of Tonduff (644 m) and Maulin (570 m).

- After about 1 km fork right, then 50 m later turn right down a narrow, overgrown path to rejoin the minor road.

- For Knockree Hostel, turn left and follow the road for 100 m.

View from Knockree Hill to the south

3·2 Glencree River to Oldbridge

Map	**panels 1 and 2**
Distance	**18 kilometres (11 miles)**
Terrain	**mainly forest tracks and mountain paths (partly on boardwalk); boggy underfoot and exposed in places**
Grade	**moderate climb and descent from Glencree River to Glensoulan, then steady ascent to White Hill (630 metres), followed by further uphill and downhill work**
Side-trip	**Djouce mountain (725 metres)**
Summary	**splendid views of loughs and mountains punctuate a day made strenuous by the gradients, terrain and extra distance to accommodation before start and after finish**

Lough Tay

Glencree River — 8 / 5 — Djouce ▲ / White Hill — 10 / 6 — Oldbridge

- At the minor road around Knockree Hill, cross over and turn right into the next bit of wood, heading west for 500 m.

- Bear left on to a path, then go over the stile and down a grassy path towards the river.

- At Glencree River, turn sharp left (south-east) to follow the tree-lined path downstream for over 1 km. At the footbridge, cross the river.

- Turn right along the path leading to a forest track that climbs away from the river. This meets the road at a T-junction where you turn left. (To reach Coolakay House, stick to this road for 700 m, turn left for 1 km, then right across the River Dargle for 1 further km, finally left for 1 km.)

Beside Glencree River

- To continue the Way, follow the road for only 300 m, turning sharp right into Crone Woods. Cross the car park and pass the gate to follow the track into the woods, soon turning left at the information board.

- Follow the waymarkers as the road zigzags uphill through the forest, with its mixture of Scots pine and beech giving way to spruce. Higher up, clear felling has left large bare areas, with the compensation of great views toward Great Sugarloaf mountain to the east. The road gradually narrows to a footpath.

- At Ride Rock, you round a corner and a wonderful view over Powerscourt Deerpark opens out beneath you, with Djouce mountain as the backdrop to Powerscourt waterfall. There's a memorial seat from which to view the waterfall, Ireland's tallest at 121 m (398 ft).

Powerscourt Waterfall, seen from the Way

- The path follows a cliff above the valley for a further 600 m, with some closer views of the waterfall. There's a dramatic rocky outcrop to climb over and handrails in places.

- Watch out for waymarkers in the next section (Glensoulan). In March 2008 recent clear felling had left little to guide you down the steep descent to the River Dargle. However you could see, far below you and to the right, a sturdy footbridge known as the 'Watergates'. So you had only to pick your way across the rocks and fallen branches to descend to the bridge.

- Once across the Dargle, which feeds Powerscourt waterfall, the Way continues south, climbing steeply along the line of a stone wall on your right, then veering left.

- One km after the Watergates, the Way turns right (south-west) across a timber stile over the wall, where there's a Wicklow mountains information board.

> ### Djouce mountain
> *Of the two paths to the summit from the Way, the southerly one is easier (100 m vertical climb) than the easterly (170 m, with a steep section near the top). Allow an extra hour for the round trip, plus time to enjoy the superb views of the coast and of Maulin and Great Sugarloaf to the north. To descend, avoid backtracking by turning left at the summit and descend southerly to rejoin the Way. Beware of the paths that descend westerly to the Coffin Stone.*

- Follow the well-trodden path, bearing left where a green track goes straight ahead. You are climbing the shoulder of Djouce mountain, passing an obvious path to its summit (725 m) on the right. On a clear day, this detour is well worth the effort: see panel.

- The Way rises climbs gently around Djouce for 1.5 km to reach a saddle that joins it to White Hill, where the descent path from Djouce's summit rejoins the Way. In clear conditions, you'll see great views, with Dublin harbour and the Howth peninsula in the north, Great Sugarloaf to the east and rolling hills to the south.

- For the next 3 km the Way runs on a raised boardwalk made from railway sleepers, to conserve the blanket bog and its vegetation. The wire netting gives secure footing, but in high cross-winds it can be hard to keep your balance.

North-east toward Great Sugarloaf, from the boardwalk

South-west toward Scarr and Tonelagee mountains

- Finally the boardwalk descends down steps into a valley called the Barr, past a memorial boulder to J B Malone, the architect of the original Wicklow Way: see page 61. There are splendid views over Lough Tay from here.

- After the memorial, follow the newer, left branch of boardwalk with handrail, veering left down a short path with overhanging low branches. This meets a forest lane where you turn right, downhill past an information board and small car park.

- Turn left at the main road and walk along the R759. (The photograph of Lough Tay on page 4 was taken from the roadside viewpoint, a detour to the right.)

- Within 1 km you reach the Pier Gates, from which you may opt for a longer detour along the private road through Luggala Estate to approach the shore of Lough Tay.

- About 300 m after the Pier Gates, the Way turns right into the forest. Follow the heather-lined forest road, bearing right uphill and soon gaining great views of the hills to your right. To your left is Vartry Reservoir, consisting of two artificial lakes at Roundwood, supplying most of South Dublin's water.

- The Way climbs around the shoulder of Sleamaine, and then drops to the saddle between it and the next hill. Follow the waymarkers south-west around the shoulder of Ballinafunshoge for a further 2 km or so.

- The forest road starts to swing left (easterly). In March 2008 the clear-felling looked recent and drastic, but it had opened up glorious views over Lough Dan, with Scarr mountain behind.

- As the road veers further left, slightly downhill, you see views of Vartry Reservoir. Don't miss the waymarker (set back, on the left), where you turn right, down a narrow gravelly path through gorse and spruce.

- The path ends at a ladder stile. Climb over and turn right to follow the field boundary downhill to a gate. If it's still padlocked, climb it at its hinges.

- Turn right to follow beside the gorse hedge and pass through a timber kissing gate. Descend the broad fenced track to cross a stile into a private lane.

- Turn right down the lane, within 300 m reaching a crossroads where the Way turns right. (If you are staying in Roundwood, leave the Way here and walk about 3 km from the crossroads to reach the village.)

Stile at foot of narrow path

Across Lough Dan to Scarr mountain

3·3 Oldbridge to Glendalough

Map	**panel 2**
Distance	**10 kilometres (6 miles)**
Terrain	**over 2.5 km of road walking, then forest track and some mountain paths, boggy in places**
Grade	**moderate gradients, maximum height 350 metres**
Side-trips	**Glendalough Monastic City**
Summary	**a short and fairly undemanding section, allowing plenty of time to visit the atmospheric Monastic City and explore the scenery and wildlife of the upper valley of Glendalough**

• At the crossroads, turn right and follow the road for about 4 km. Just after crossing the River Avonmore, you reach this junction at Oldbridge with many signs. (To reach Lough Dan House, turn right here and walk uphill for about 2 km.) The Way bears left, soon passing the Wicklow Way Lodge, and climbs steeply up a spur of Scarr mountain.

• The road descends and rises again before reaching Wart Stone field, 2.5 km after Oldbridge, where you turn right. The name is from a hollowed-out stone or *bullaun* in which water collected. It was believed to cure warts.

Signpost at Oldbridge road junction

The Way crossing the shoulder of Paddock Hill

- Follow the rough track uphill for five minutes or so, up a boreen, over the stile and through the farm gates. You reach the cow byre at Brusher Gate, with fine views behind you: see the photograph on page 26.

- Cross two stiles roughly at right angles, turning left (south) to cross Paddock Hill.

- Follow the clear path alongside the wall, at first beside a young plantation, then across open hillside, to reach another patch of forest.

- Soon the path starts its descent, giving fine views over Laragh and the hills around the Vale of Glendalough. The path descends steeply in places, swinging right and dropping to the Sally Gap road (R115).

- Cross the road, turning left. After 200 m, turn right down a path which descends to Glenmacnass River and crosses it by a timber footbridge.

- On its far side, turn right (unless diverting for accommodation in Laragh) and follow the well-made path amongst the Scots pines.

- At first the path wanders upstream near the river, then it bends away uphill. Soon it meets a forest road where you turn right, immediately passing over a crossroads and later following a hairpin bend uphill, with open views to your left.

Rolling hills and good grazing near Oldbridge

Oldbridge		Brusher Gate		Glendalough
	4		6	
	2½		3½	

- Immediately after, turn left off the road (which sweeps right) and leave the forest over a stile.

- Follow the path which emerges to a superb view over the two lakes of Glendalough, with the Round Tower and St Kevin's Church clearly visible.

- Look out for a sharp left turn down a path that descends very steeply at first, down through the trees.

- Exit Brockagh Forest, passing over four stiles in quick succession, then cross a stream and fifth stile to reach the Wicklow Gap road (R756).

- Cross straight over the road and follow a short boreen down to meet the next road opposite the Glendalough Hotel. Turn left here (unless aiming for the youth hostel, to the right). The Glendalough Visitor Centre is on your right side, just beyond the hotel buildings.

- The Way passes the entrance to the Visitor Centre, which is well worth a visit: see panel on page 20. Afterwards, cross the Glendasan River by a footbridge, from which you'll see the view shown on our front cover.

View over Glendalough from the Way

Map	panels 2 and 3
Distance	16 kilometres (10 miles)
Terrain	mainly forest tracks and mountain paths, boggy underfoot in places but partly on boardwalk; no public road walking
Grade	moderate zigzagging climb to 570 metres (the saddle below Mullacor) then a longish descent to Glenmalure
Summary	a mainly woodland walk with fine wildlife and waterfalls and splendid mountain views

Poulanass waterfall

Glendalough 9 6 Saddle 7 4 Glenmalure

- Turn right at the signpost for the Green Road towards the Upper Lake. After 200 m a sign points right across a footbridge into the Monastic City. Allow at least an hour to enjoy this wonderful place: see page 20.

- The Way goes straight on past the Lower Lake, where there's a National Park Information Centre. (Beyond it lies a car park with toilets.) Turn left across a footbridge and climb the steep path with flights of steps alongside Lugduff Brook and Poulanass waterfall. Its green water is shown in the photograph on page 29.

- Above the top flight of steps, the path meets a forest track. Turn left up the track and left again to cross two bridges and round a bend. (Between the two bridges a panel displays five kinds of rock found in the Wicklow mountains: see page 28.) You are now heading north-east and may glimpse the car park below, through the trees.

- About 600 m after the bridges, turn sharp right (south) and follow the track for 1.5 km up the steep western shoulder of Derrybawn mountain. (Look behind you to glimpse the upper lake.) Cross Lugduff Brook again, swinging right.

The Way climbing Derrybawn mountain

- The Way now heads generally south-west and west, uphill for about 3 km. Check carefully for waymarkers at the next three junctions, until you emerge from the forest to reach the saddle between two mountains: Lugduff (652 m) and Mullacor (657 m).

Fraughan Rock Glen, from Mullacor saddle

- From here, look south-west for Fraughan Rock Glen and Lugnaquillia beyond. At 925 m, the 'Lug' is the highest of the Wicklow mountains.

- At the saddle, the path turns sharp left along the edge of a boggy section. Cross the bog on a boardwalk made of sleepers, heading south-west, then briefly south-east, around the shoulder of Mullacor mountain.

- The boardwalk slopes downhill and curves to the left, soon giving way to a path which runs above the forest for about 200 m. Watch out for a waymarker pointing down a steep rocky path into dense forest, apt to be boggy in places. Down this you descend into the valley of Glenmalure.

- After 500 m you meet a good forest road, where you turn left. After about 1 km there's an Adirondack timber shelter, handy for a break or even, at a pinch, overnight. It's set back discreetly among the trees on your left: see the photograph on page 17.

- The Way descends south-easterly, and after a final twist, reaches the tarmac road. Here you turn right (south-west), soon to reach the cross-roads and facilities of Drumgoff (Glenmalure Lodge).

- If staying at the Glenmalure An Óige Hostel, turn right at this cross-roads and walk about 6 km up the valley – or, if you can find the track down from the 'good forest road' (mentioned above) to the car park below, save yourself up to two hours of doubling back: see drop-down map.

Carrawaystick waterfall, from the Way

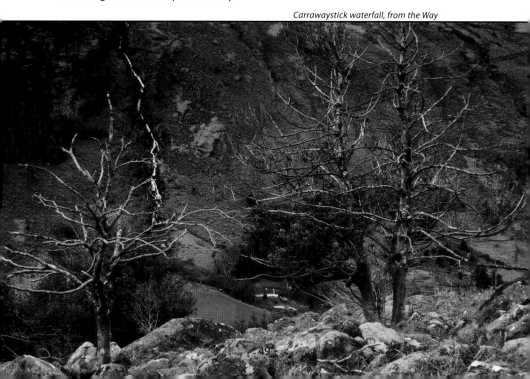

3·5 Glenmalure to Iron Bridge

Map	**panel 3**
Distance	**14 kilometres (9 miles)**
Terrain	**mixture of forest roads, rough tracks and boggy paths; very little roadside walking (7%)**
Grade	**steady climb out of Glenmalure up shoulder of Slieve Maan, some descent followed by ascent almost to the summit of Carrickashane (508 m), then descent to the Ow Valley**
Summary	**although only a modest distance, this part of the Way is hilly and may be slow going, especially in the wet; the section ends too far from Aughrim for it to be sensible or safe to walk there**

Glenmalure scenery

- Return to the crossroads and continue south-west to cross the Avonbeg River. On your left stand the ruins of Drumgoff Barracks, built in about 1803 as part of the British effort to control the Wicklow wilderness, but used only briefly. By the 1830s it had been sold to miners.

- Just afterwards, turn right to cross Clohernagh Brook by a concrete bridge. The duck-boards are intended for emergency crossing when the Brook is in spate, and there's now a metal handrail.

Halfway obelisk

- Walk towards the forest gate, noting the granite obelisk: you have now reached the official halfway point, although you will have walked further than the 63.5 km (39.5 miles). The Way bears left and climbs steadily by means of clearly waymarked zigzags.

- After two left turns, the track dips to cross the Clohernagh Brook again, and then turns left once more.

- Walk east for 1 km, then turn sharp right up a narrow path which climbs steeply (south-westerly) up the ridge of Slieve Maan mountain. Follow this path for 1 km, ignoring the forest track which it crosses, until it levels out.

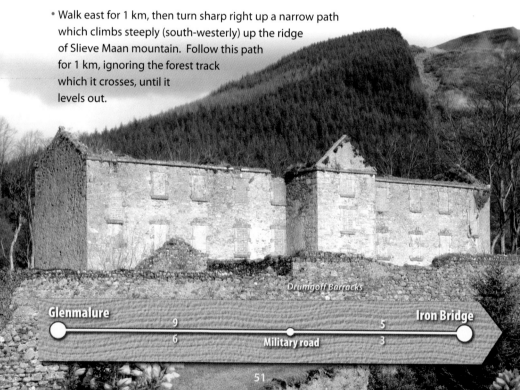

Drumgoff Barracks

Glenmalure 9 6 Military road 3 5 Iron Bridge

Dense mosses flourish in the damp forest

- Turn left slightly downhill, then shortly turn right up a good forest road. This runs westerly at first, then veers south-south-west for about 1.5 km.

- After a couple of zigzags, look for the turn left down a rough path through the trees, descending to open bog. Follow the path as it meanders and turns right along an old fence.

- When you reach the Military Road, turn right. After 200 m, turn left along a forest track.

- The track climbs for 1 km or so, at first through clear-felled forest, almost to the summit of Carrickashane mountain (508 m). Turn right down a steep, muddy path. If you are lucky, you may enjoy more views of Lugnaquillia.

- At a wide forest road, turn diagonally left and continue downhill. At a Y-junction, bear right and descend to the minor road.

- Turn right down the road, then left down a rough track to a T-junction. Turn right along the road to cross the Ow River at Iron Bridge, where peaty water falls over the rocks in rapids.

- Once across the river, turn sharp left along the Aughrim Road for 500 m.

- Bear right up a forest road to reach a very minor road where you turn left, shortly arriving at Ballyteige Bridge. Here the Way leaves the road, keeping right where the road swings left for Askanagap.

- If your accommodation is in Aughrim, 9 km away, you'll need to have arranged for collection from Iron Bridge or Ballyteige Bridge.

Steep. muddy path with hiker above

3·6 Iron Bridge to Tinahely

Map	**panel 4**
Distance	**21 kilometres (13 miles)**
Terrain	**forest track, grassy lanes and rather a lot of road-walking (33%)**
Grade	**rolling hills have gentler gradients, but the pattern of rise and fall between valleys is unchanged**
Summary	**attractive views of rolling countryside from a mixture of lanes, roads and tracks; splendid wild flowers in spring; section finishes 2 km short of the Georgian village of Tinahely**

- From Ballyteige Bridge, walk into the woodland and follow the track uphill (west) for 2 km. Near the top, from the shoulder of Sheilstown Hill, you glimpse a view to the west through the trees.

- Turn left to descend an undulating path with fine open views to your right. After 1 km, the Way zigzags right, left and right again before reaching the minor road.

Open views from Sheilstown Hill

Iron Bridge   9   5   R747 to Tinahely
     6   Moyne   3   Ford   7   4

The lane descends to St Colmcille's Well

- Turn left and follow the road for 3 km, ignoring two roads that join you from the right. (However, if staying at Jigsaw Cottage, Moyne, turn right steeply downhill at the second of these, after 2.5 km of minor road.)

- Shortly (800 m) after the Moyne turning, the road swings sharply left, but you turn right down a lane which meets another road within 700 m.

- Turn left to continue the Way. You may wish first to divert about 50 m to the right to see the Holy Well (dedicated to St Colmcille, or St Columba) on the far side of the road, sadly even more overgrown than in the photograph below.

- About 150 m after the junction, turn sharp right to descend via Rathshanmore Road to the river, which you cross at Sandyford Bridge.

- Immediately after, turn left along a very minor road running parallel to the river along its narrow valley for nearly 3 km. The hills on your right are Ballycumber (North and South) and on your left, Slieveroe. In spring, the hedgerow is a mass of wild flowers.

- Keep left at the complicated junction, and turn left again at the ruins of an old school.

St Colmcille's Well

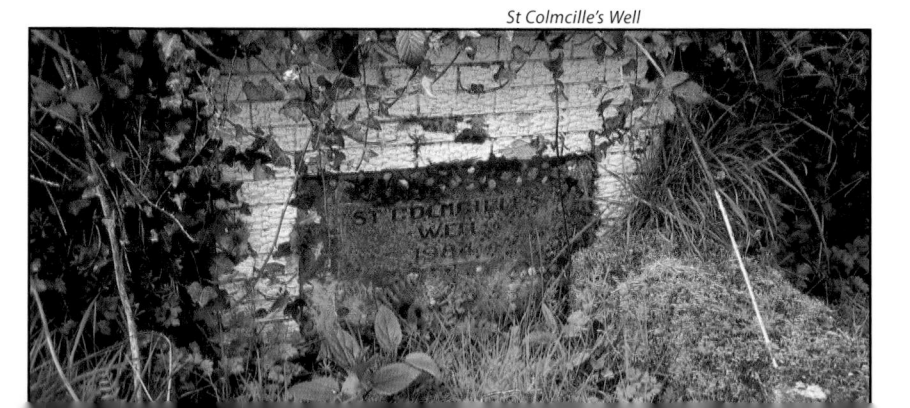

The Way fords a small river

- Follow the winding road downhill, and just before a bridge, turn right to ford the river by means of stepping stones. Follow the lane which climbs uphill, leading to a narrow boreen in which wild flowers flourish in spring.

- Pass through the gate and continue along the boreen. About 1 km after the ford, you pass an overgrown pre-historic rath on your right: see page 62. Continue along the line of the boreen, keeping the stone wall on your left.

- Soon after a stone cross (a memorial to a doctor killed in a shooting accident) you bear right uphill and follow the line of another wall.

- Turn right at a T-junction and continue through a gate into a plantation, following signs to turn left among the trees of Coolafunshoge Wood. Descend to the edge of the forest and leave it through the gate.

- Turn right into the lane (Coolafunshoge Lane) and follow it through several gates at intervals over the next 2 km. You can see Tinahely below you, but it feels a long time before you reach the end of this lane at a T-junction and turn right to cross the Derry River by a concrete footbridge.

- At the main road (R747), turn left and walk along the roadside. After 300 m, the Way turns off sharply right. To reach the centre of Tinahely, continue along this road for nearly 2 km.

3·7 Tinahely to Clonegal

Map	**panels 4 and 5**
Distance	**31 kilometres (20 miles)**
Terrain	**63% of this distance involves road walking (82% to Raheenakit, then 47% to Clonegal), with some respite on grassy lanes and forest tracks**
Grade	**undulating countryside makes for fairly gentle gradients**
Side-trips	**Huntington Castle**
Summary	**this section could be split by overnighting at Shillelagh (which adds to the road-walking), or tackled as a single long day**

- To resume the Way from Tinahely, walk 1.6 km north-west along the R747 to where the Way bears left (north-west) up a minor road. After 750 m, turn hard left up a narrow, very overgrown boreen, an ancient drove road for cattle (beware of brambles and nettles).

- After the short boreen, turn left uphill to follow a wide, gorse-lined boreen along the shoulder of Muskeagh Hill (see photograph on page 6). This teems with flowers and insects, and offers fine views to your right (west).

- The path swings round and you join a lane which descends to meet a road where you turn left. After nearly 1 km, turn right towards Mullinacuff.

View west from Muskeagh Hill

- Within 250 m you reach a staggered junction: cross the road from Shillelagh to Hacketstown, and then turn left almost immediately.

- After a further 1.5 km you reach Stranakelly Crossroads where there is a wonderful pub. Although the sign outside shows the name 'Tallons', it is known as the 'Dying Cow', and is well worth a visit (see panel).

- Turn sharp right at the crossroads and follow the road for 4 km, after 1.5 km passing the Lugnaquillia View B&B.

- The road ascends quite steeply at first, then undulates around the lower slopes of Cronelea Hill with good views to the north.

- After descending to the T-junction, turn sharp left along the slightly wider road, passing a church and a few houses halfway to the junction with the main road to Shillelagh (R725).

- Cross the road at a staggered junction, basically keeping straight on steeply uphill, but soon reaching a T-junction with another minor road: turn left. In spring, these hedgerows are brilliant with wildflowers.

Rich farmland below Muskeagh Hill

> ℹ️ **The Dying Cow**
> This pub gained its name during hard times, when the widow who ran it was challenged by the gardaí (police) for serving alcohol after hours. Her defence was that she was only serving friends helping her with her 'dying cow'. The name has stuck since 1916. Hot and cold drinks, no food but picnicking permitted

Wild flowers flourish in the hedgerows

R747 to Tinahely				Clonegal
8	6	12	5	
5 'Dying Cow'	4 Raheenakit	8	'dog-leg' 3	

- After just over 1 km of descent, watch for the right turn uphill. (The junction with the R725 at Boley Bridge is just below you.) The road climbs steeply at first, then undulates, and has fine open views to your left (east).

- Near its top, watch for where the Way turns right over the brow of a hill along the second track into the forest at Raheenakit. The name means the 'fort of the cat', recalling the time before wildcats became extinct in Ireland.

- If heading for accommodation in Shillelagh, instead continue straight on past Raheenakit for 700 m to Ballard Crossroads, where you turn left and walk 2 km to the village.

- After the Way turns right into Raheenakit forest, the trees are set well back and you enjoy wide views south over Counties Wexford and Carlow. Within 250 m, turn right uphill among tall Scots pines, following the path as it curves left and does a right-then-left turn.

- About 1 km after leaving the road, the Way turns right (north-westerly).

- The Way now follows three sides of a rectangle to maintain its direction: within 250 m turn right uphill, then left and left again at the T-junction. Finally the Way swings right, continuing north-westerly and levelling out.

- Look for a left turn over a stile down a grassy lane. This is easily missed because the waymarker is beyond the stile and the lane looks informal. Follow it as it winds downhill, turning right at the junction with a track, passing a farmhouse. Descend further to a road, where the Way turns right.

Easily-missed turning: the Way passes over the stile

- The Way is about to meander at length around Moylisha and Urelands Hills. If short of time, consider an unofficial shortcut: instead turn sharp left along the road and walk south toward New Bridge. After 1 km turn right steeply up an ungated farm road (ignoring the gated field entrance to its right). This swings south, soon becoming a tarmac road, which after a further 1.5 km reaches a T-junction. Turn right for just over 1 km to rejoin the Way at the 'dog-leg' mentioned at the fifth bullet below.

- To stick to the Way, 500 m after turning right along the road, turn left uphill for 1 km. This road has very fine hedgerows.

- Turn left at the T-junction and follow that road for 1 km, until directed off left, through a gate into woodland. You ascend steeply in places, alongside a stream and wall, veering north-east.

- The Way turns sharp right, and follows the ridge southward for over 1 km, with fine views to your right and, in summer, lots of butterflies.

- After a long zigzagging descent, turn left at the very minor road, along its corridor of beeches. Cross the next road in a 'dog-leg', bearing left then right.

- Within 2 km you reach Wicklow Bridge, a junction where a signpost announces Clonegal as 3 km to your right.

- This road reaches Clonegal at a junction near a green with an inscribed stone and flowers: see page 9. In 2006 a stone bench and information board were placed opposite the green to mark the terminus of the Way.

> **Huntington Castle**
> Built in 1625, this superb Jacobean castle includes granite stones and oak beams from an earlier castle on the same site. It was built by the First Lord Esmonde and is still home to his direct descendants. Open afternoons daily June to August, Sundays only in September. Guided tours EUR 5, tel (0) 54 77 552

Huntington Castle, Clonegal

Clonegal has attractive late Georgian and Victorian houses and shop fronts, with many historical associations. Turn left after the green, downhill towards the river. You pass the entrance drive to Huntington Castle: see panel on page 59.

The fine bridge over the Derry River has a plaque that commemorates the 1798 rebellion. Beyond it lies a smaller settlement called Watch House Village.

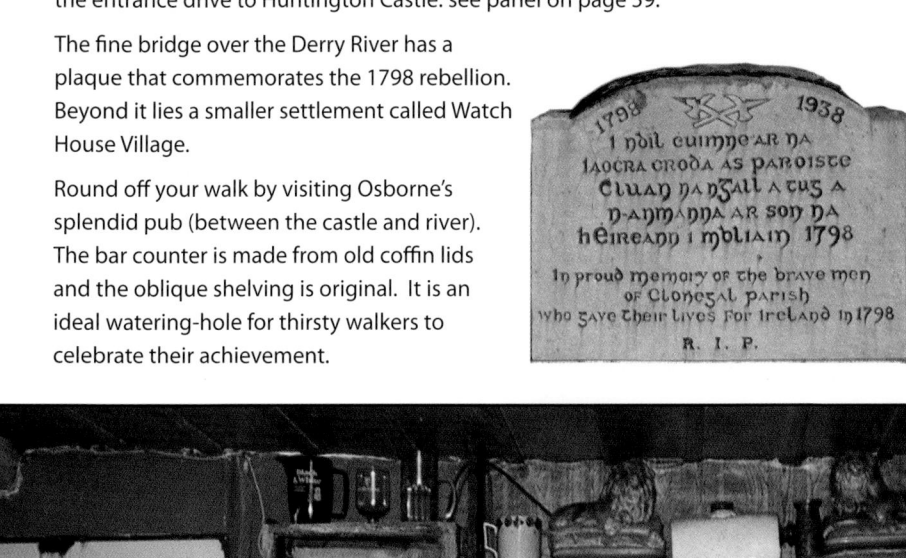

1798 1938

I nDil cuimne ar na
laocra croda as paroiste
Cluan na ngall a tug a
n-anmanna ar son na
hEireann i mbliain 1798

In proud memory of the brave men
of Clonegal parish
who gave their lives for Ireland in 1798

R. I. P.

Round off your walk by visiting Osborne's splendid pub (between the castle and river). The bar counter is made from old coffin lids and the oblique shelving is original. It is an ideal watering-hole for thirsty walkers to celebrate their achievement.

GUINNESS
IS GOOD
FOR YOU

HARP
Cool
Satisfaction

GUINNESS

GUINNESS

PERRI

With 6,000
VFI Pubs outside
of Dublin...

SHAMROCK
SWEEP

PIKAY

Inside Osborne's antique pub

Reference

Development of the Wicklow Way

The late J B Malone, a legendary figure in Irish hill-walking, first published his scheme for a Wicklow Way in 1966. His circular route then returned to Dublin via the mountains of west Wicklow.

In 1978 he was employed by Cospoir, the National Sports Council, to implement it as a linear walk to Clonegal. From there a 4-km road walk to Kildavin links to the South Leinster Way, a further part of the E8 footpath which is to link Dursey Island, Co Kerry, with Istanbul, Turkey.

In 1980, the Wicklow Way was opened as far as Luggala, and in 1982 extended to Clonegal, becoming Ireland's first and best-known Waymarked Way. Malone's *Complete Wicklow Way* was published in 1988 by O'Brien Press. The Way's 25-year jubilee was celebrated in 2006 when some information boards and stone landmarks were installed. The Way is now managed by the Wicklow Trails Committee.

The Irish name for the Way appears on many signposts: see title page. *Slí Cualann Nua* means literally the 'new Cuala Way'. The old *Slí Cualann* was one of the five great roads radiating from Tara in ancient Ireland, running through the Land of Cuala, now Wicklow.

Further reading

Bardwell, S et al *Walking in Ireland* 2nd ed Lonely Planet 2003 1-86450-323-8
Comprehensive and useful for planning circular and shorter walks; new edition, likely in 2009

Fewer, M *The Wicklow Military Road: History and Topography* Ashfield Press 2007 978-1-901658-66-8
A detailed, illustrated account, of interest to walkers with a sense of history.

Key websites

The most helpful website on the Wicklow Way is **www.wicklowway.com** which carries up-to-date information on accommodation and travel; it also lists facilities in each village and is the best single source of links: highly recommended.

Fáilte Ireland, the Irish Tourist Board, has a website aimed at visitors in general. It's useful for travel to and within Ireland, and lets you browse and book accommodation and/or choose a tour operator: **www.discoverireland.ie.**

The general tourism website for County Wicklow is **www.visitwicklow.ie** and the Wicklow Uplands Council's site is **www.wicklowuplands.ie**

All Irish Waymarked Ways are listed, together with a list of events and festivals, at **www.walkireland.ie**

Memorial to J B Malone: see page 42

Service providers

Footfalls Walking Holidays
www.walkinghikingireland.com
Irish Ways   www.irishways.com
SouthWestWalks Ireland
www.southwestwalksireland.com
Trek-Inn   www.trek-inn.com
Tailor-made Tours   www.tailor-madetours.com
Wicklow Way Baggage
www.wicklowwaybaggage.com
Wonderful Ireland   www.wonderfulireland.com

Weather forecasts

The Irish Meteorological Service (Met Éirann) has a helpful website at **www.met.ie** or phone Weatherdial on 1550 123 814 (Leinster, i.e. most of the Way) or 1550 123 817 for the Dublin area.

Hostels and camping

An Óige (the Irish Youth Hostel Association) is at 61 Mountjoy Street, Dublin 7 (tel 00 353 1 830 4555). Hostels are shown on its map *Budget Accommodation in Ireland*. You can book online on the website **www.anoige.ie**. In addition to Dublin, it has three hostels close to the route: Knockree and Glendalough (open all year) and Glenmalure (open July/August only in 2008). Membership is not required, although it brings discounts on hostel charges, travel *et al*. Overnight charges vary according to location and season, in 2008 ranging from €15 (Glenmalure) to about €20-25 (Knockree, Glendalough) or a little more for Dublin International in high season.

Independent Holiday Hostels of Ireland
www.hostels-ireland.com has a wide choice of hostels in Dublin.

The Irish Caravan & Camping Council, PO Box 4443, Dublin 2 maintains lists of campsites with gradings. Prices vary: in 2008 Roundwood Caravan Park (open May-August) charged €12-13 per person for hikers with tents. The website is
www.camping-ireland.ie

Transport

Aer Lingus	www.aerlingus.com
Ryanair	www.ryanair.com
Dublin Airport	www.dublinairport.com
easyJet	www.easyJet.com
Bus Éireann	www.buseireann.ie
Dublin Bus	www.dublinbus.ie
St Kevins Bus Service	
	www.glendaloughbus.com
Irish Rail	www.irishrail.ie
DART (rapid transit)	
	www.dublin.ie/transport/dart

Glossary

boreen	old, narrow country lane
bullaun stones	hollowed-out stones often found near early Christian sites; perhaps used as a mortar, or for making altar bread
garda, gardai	police (singular, plural)
gleann (glen)	valley, usually U-shaped
green road	old country road with no tarmac (bitumen) and sometimes a grassy surface
mass path	path created by Catholics during times of persecution while walking to secret places for Mass
rath	fort or defended dwelling, roughly circular, often dating from the Iron Age or later (500 BC onward)

Pronunciation guide

Place stress on the syllable shown in **bold**. Visitors to Ireland often find pronunciation difficult. Try asking a native to demonstrate, then practise: this may provide innocent amusement all round.

An Óige	an **oyig**a
Aughrim	**och** rim
Bunclody	bun **cload**ee
Céad míle fáilte	kaid meela **fawl**cha
Coolafunshoge	coolafun **showg**
Coillte	**kwillt** sha
Djouce	jowss
Dun Laoghaire	doun **leer**y
Fáilte	**fawl** cha
Fir (male toilet)	fear
Gardaí (police)	**gard**ee
Glendalough	glenn da loch
Kilmashogue	kilma **showg**
Lugnaquillia	lugna **kwill** ya
Mná (female toilet)	mi **naw**
Slí Cualann Nua	shlee **kooal**an **noo**ah
Tinahely	tina **heel**y

Notes for novices

If you lack experience in walking long distances, you may find our notes on preparation and gear helpful. They are available free to website visitors as a download from **www.rucsacs.com**. If you can't access this, send a suitably stamped addressed envelop marked 'Notes for novices' to:

Rucksack Readers, Landrick Lodge, Dunblane, FK15 0HY, UK.

Maps

The Ordnance Survey Ireland Discovery Series (1:50,000) covers almost the entire Way in three sheets, except for Clonegal which falls just outside sheet 62. In April 2008, the latest editions were sheet 50 (2007), sheet 56 (2007) and sheet 62 (2003). Check for new editions before buying.

Harvey's *Wicklow Mountains* map covers the northern part of the Way (from pp 37-49) in more detail (1:30,000) than OSI sheet 56. It's recommended for hill-walking in Wicklow, but obtain the 2nd edition (2008): the previous edition showed the route incorrectly near Roundwood.

The latest editions of these maps are available direct from **www.rucsacs.com**.

Acknowledgements

The author is grateful for the following for support, for expert local information, and for many improvements to the second edition: Sandra Bardwell, Mary Brophy, the Bray Strollers, Sean and Theresa Byrne, Leslie Gilmour, Marilyn Kinlan, Helen Lawless, Joss Lynam, Susan McGann, Kevin Megarry, Richard More-O'Ferrall and Eoin Reilly. None of these is responsible for any opinions expressed, nor for any failings that may remain.

Picture credits

Uto Hogerzeil p21 (syluto@indigo.ie); **Sandra Bardwell** p28, p40 (upper), p48 (lower), p61; **Fáilte Ireland** p8, p13 (lower), p50; **Johnnie Fox's Pub** p5 (lower); **P Cairns/www.stockscotland.com** p32; **Forest Life Picture Library** p33 (upper); **Jacquetta Megarry** front cover, p1 (both), p4, p6, p7 (all 4), p11, p13 (upper), p14, p16 (all), p22 (both), p23, p24 (both), p25, p26 (both), p29 (both), p30, p31, p33 (lower), p34, p35, p36 (both), p37, p 38, p39, p40 (lower), p41 (both), p42, p43 (both), p44 (both), p45, p46, p47, p48 (upper), p51 (both), p52 (both), p53, p54 (both), p55, p56, p57 (both), p58, p59, p60 (both), back cover; **Eoin Reilly** p17 (lower), p36 (lower), p49; **Roundwood Campsite** p17 (upper).

Rucksack Readers

Rucksack Readers has published books covering long-distance walks in Scotland, Ireland and worldwide (the Alps, China, Peru and Tanzania). There's also a Rucksack Pocket Summits series for climbers of the world's 'seven summits'. For more information, or to order online, visit **www.rucsacs.com**. To order by telephone, dial 01786 824 696 (+44 1786 824 696).

978-1-898481-21-8

978-1-898481-24-9

978-1-898481-29-4

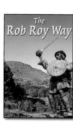

978-1-898481-26-3

978-1-898481-27-0

978-1-898481-30-0

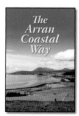

978-1-898481-28-7

978-1-898481-18-8

978-1-898481-22-5

978-1-898481-25-6

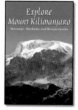

978-1-898481-23-2

978-1-898481-20-1

Index